NOV22

cover TO cover BIBLE STUDY

GROUP

The Covenants

GOD'S PROMISES AND THEIR RELEVANCE TODAY

CWR

John Houghton

Published 2003 by CWR, Waverley Abbey House, Waverley Lane, Farnham, Surrey GU9 8EP, UK. Registered Charity No. 294387.
Registered Limited Company No. 1990308. Reprinted 2004, 2013, 2019.

For a list of National Distributors, visit cwr.org.uk/distributors

Concept development, editing, design and production by CWR.

Front cover image: Roger Walker.

Printed in the UK by Linney.

ISBN: 978-1-85345-255-0

Contents

Introduction

This series of homegroup studies is about the way God reveals Himself and deals with us by means of a series of covenants. There is nothing mysterious about the term. Covenants are commonplace in our human experience; they are the way that we establish a basis for trust and understanding in our dealings with one another, especially if the deal is long-term.

The most common covenants that people enter into are marriage, property purchase and trading partnerships. In each of these cases the two parties commit themselves freely to mutually-agreed terms within the prevailing law and all covenants of this kind can properly be terminated if the conditions are breached by one or both parties. Adultery, desertion and cruelty are accepted as grounds for divorce because they constitute a breaking of the covenant to love and to cherish exclusively for a lifetime. A failure to pay the mortgage will soon end your covenant with the building society or bank! Likewise, a business partnership will come to an end if one partner is proven dishonest or fails to deliver what was promised.

Humans break their covenants through weakness, greed and perversity. However, God never breaks His. Once He has made a covenant He sticks to it, relentlessly and passionately. That can be for us the source of greatest comfort and encouragement but it can also be quite scary! How God behaves towards His covenants reveals to us something of the awesome holiness of His character and the depth of His commitment.

Perhaps this is why God does not let us make up our own covenants with Him. He is always the initiator and He is the One who sets the terms and conditions. Unlike human covenants we do not have an equal say, nor do we have equal

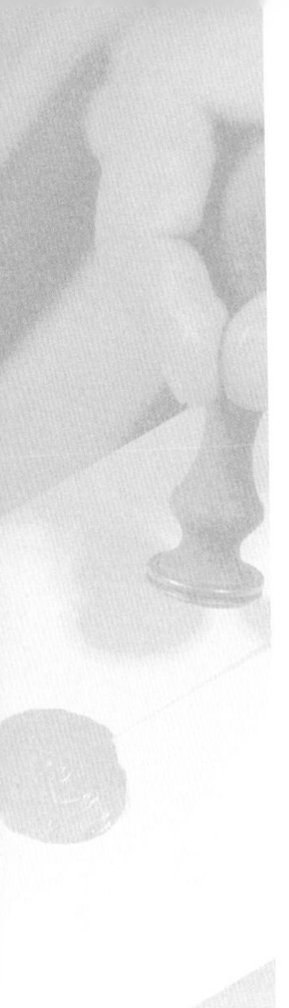

obligations. God's covenants are not 'fair shares for all', but they are always good. Left to ourselves we would make covenants based upon self-interest, whereas God, being full of love for those made in His image, always makes covenants with our best interests at heart.

We shall be looking together at seven covenants but, of course, our Bibles are divided into two parts, the Old Testament and New Testament. *Testamentum* is the Latin translation of *diatheke,* which is the Greek word for covenant. The Hebrew word is *berith*. This division of our Bibles reminds us that the coming of Christ introduced a new covenant that superseded the old covenant given through Moses. As the apostle John puts it: 'For the law was given through Moses; grace and truth came through Jesus Christ' (John 1:17).

This does not mean that we should dismiss part one of our Bibles! Not only does the Old Testament contain much that is new covenant but it is actually quite impossible to understand the New Testament without reading the Old Testament. Furthermore, some aspects of the Old Testament covenants still apply to all of us in our contemporary world.

In my series of children's books, *The Oswain Tales,* I introduced, as a metaphor for the Bible, a magical book called *The Tale of the Seven Rainbows*. To help us remember the different covenants I have colour-coded them in this study using the colours of the rainbow, though not in the order that they appear in the rainbow's spectrum. Let me say at once that this is purely to help our memories and no one should build a theology around my colour selection or read anything further into the meaning of the colours themselves!

The first is God's self-covenant and it springs from His deepest nature. God is love and He expresses that love in what we call covenant love. I have chosen the colour green because of the emerald rainbow that surrounds His throne in Revelation 4:3. The second is the covenant with Adam and I have gone for the colour orange to remind us of the fruit of the tree in the Garden of Eden. The third covenant is with Noah and I have selected blue with reference to the water, of which there was rather a lot! The fourth is indigo to recall the night sky when God made His covenant with Abraham. The fifth is yellow to indicate the desert wilderness where God made a covenant with Moses and the Israelites after their escape from Egypt. The sixth covenant was made with King David and I have chosen violet to remind us of his royal robes. The seventh is the covenant of grace made through our Lord Jesus Christ and it is coloured red because of His blood shed on the cross.

As with others in this series these studies are ideal for small group use. Each consists of an opening icebreaker related to the theme of the study, followed by the content of the session. There are a number of questions for discussion within the group and short sections on Personal Application and Seeing Jesus in the Scriptures to round off the session. There is a section of Leader's Notes to assist in the leading of the group.

No Bible study should be for mere information; it is important that you pray through the truths under consideration and that you seek to relate them to your own life and situation. Although these covenants were established many centuries ago they still determine the course of human history and are as relevant today as they ever were when they were first given. I hope you discover this for yourself as you study the material.

WEEK ONE

Green - *The God of Covenant Love*

Opening Icebreaker

Each take a piece of card and draw five lines crossways at random angles. Cut the cards lengthways. Keeping one half, place the other in a bowl. Then each take a random half from the bowl and find the person with the matching half.

Bible Readings

- Psalm 25:6–14; 89:3, 24–29, 34
- Isaiah 54:9–10
- Jeremiah 31:3
- Hebrews 1:1–5

Focus: God is passionately committed to keeping His Word because of His self-covenant.

Opening Our Eyes

There are many kinds of gods and many kinds of idols in the world. What kind of god do we believe in? If we are Bible believers we will at once answer that there is only one true and living God, and He is God from everlasting to everlasting. His very name, Yahweh, means 'I am who I am – the ever being One'. Idols are the constructs of human imagination and fear but God has no need for us to verify or vindicate His existence, 'for from him and through him and to him are all things'. He is the Mystery behind all the mysteries and the Source of all things. We may call Him our God but we neither possess nor control Him.

God is all-seeing, all-knowing and all-powerful; He is the Creator of all things and thus perfect in wisdom and knowledge and power. In the light of the revelation of God in Jesus Christ we will go further: God is love. He has demonstrated that love not only providentially in His general beneficence towards the world and humanity in particular, but especially in the sacrifice of His own dear Son for our salvation.

These two aspects of God's love, His love for all and His particular love for some, are distinguished in the Old Testament by two Hebrew words: *ahabah* and *chesed*. *Ahabah* is unconditional love; it is that fundamental goodwill of God towards His creation that reveals itself in everything from the reliability of the laws of physics to the pleasure enjoyed by a family on a summer beach holiday. God's *ahabah* means that goodness is the fundamental vibration of the universe.

Chesed is a particular aspect of God's love. We may translate it as covenant love; in our English Bibles it is variously rendered as loving-kindness, mercy, steadfast love. Isaiah 54:10 is one of many examples.

At the heart of covenant love is a sense of zeal, passion and keenness. It means that when God makes covenants He is utterly and faithfully, and particularly, committed in love to fulfilling them. Married love provides us with a human parallel: I may love all people in general and seek their well being – that is *ahabah* – but there is one woman whom I love not simply more than the rest, nor just in a uniquely romantic and sexual manner, but zealously. I am covenanted to my wife and so I love her with covenant love, *chesed*.

We tend to think of our marriage covenants as promises made to someone else. However, such covenants are vulnerable because they depend on the quality of our own characters to keep those promises. God, however, is covenanted to Himself, that is, He is so committed to His own inner integrity that it is inconceivable that He would ever act capriciously or dishonestly or with less than perfection. The word, the will, the heart and the ability all agree. So covenant is not something bolted onto God for our benefit. It is in the essence of His nature. We catch a hint of this in Hebrews 6:13 in respect of the covenant with Abraham where, 'since there was no-one greater for him to swear by, he swore by himself'. 'God cannot disown himself' (2 Tim. 2:13). When John catches a glimpse of heaven he sees an emerald rainbow and that may remind us of the evergreen nature of our covenant God.

Discussion Starters

1. Living as we do in a pluralistic society, how would you 'sell' your God in the marketplace of ideas?

2. Hebrews 1:3 speaks of Jesus 'sustaining all things by his powerful word'. What do you think this means?

3. God is love and God is good. How can that be so in a world full of evil?

4. People often treat God as an impotent but kindly old man. In the light of Song of Solomon 2:8–14 and 8:6–7 how would you describe God?

5. We need people of passion in the Church. Many start well but wane. What do you think causes a decline in spiritual passion? How would you remedy it?

6. The Bible describes God's people as 'saints'. What are the most important marks of 'saintliness'?

7. Many people don't marry today because they fear making a commitment they can't guarantee keeping. What do you think is the secret of a lasting marriage?

8. God's covenant with Jesus means that He has made Christ to be His heir. What do you think that means?

9. When Jesus became sin for us the Father had to turn His face away but it never broke the covenant with His Son. Why do you think we so easily doubt our Heavenly Father's ongoing commitment to us?

10. The resurrection of Christ is the ultimate fulfilment of God's covenant promise to save the world through Him. How would you explain this to a Jewish friend?

Personal Application

'You can't trust anyone nowadays.' Well, you can trust God! And if you can trust God, you can become trustworthy yourself. God's zeal is contagious; it transforms our lives producing godly devotion and wholehearted faithfulness. The Old Testament calls such people *chasidim,* holy ones or saints, a word the New Testament uses to describe all true followers of Jesus.

Covenant love is 'loyal love' – an apt term in a day of short-term commitments based upon the duration of good feelings. Reflect on how much your love for God and your fellow travellers demonstrates the loyal love of God.

Should God reflect on Himself He always finds total integrity. Spiritual maturity is about reaching such a place ourselves. Psalm 86:11 will help you.

Seeing Jesus in the Scriptures

Jesus is the special object of God's covenant love. His awareness of a unique covenant relationship with the Father defines His life and ministry. Read His baptismal affirmation in Luke 3:22. He speaks on numerous occasions of that relationship and of His own loyal commitment to it, eg John 4:34. When, in John 10:30, Jesus says 'I and the Father are one', He is making not only a statement of divinity but also a declaration of an unbreakable covenant bond.

The bond was tested to breaking point when Jesus on the cross endured separation from His Father and uttered His terrible cry (Mark 15:34). Yet God's covenant love remained firm (see Acts 2:27). Peter proclaimed that Christ is risen from the dead because of God's oath, ie covenant, that He would raise Him – so He has!

WEEK TWO

Orange - *The Covenant of Life*

Opening Icebreaker

Each member of the group has to describe a fruit without saying what it is or making it too obvious, eg don't say it's orange unless it *isn't* an orange. The others have to guess the name of the fruit.

Bible Readings

- Genesis 1:26–31; 2:15–17; 3:14–24
- Romans 5:12–19

Key verse: Genesis 1:28

Focus: God has purposed blessing for the entire human race.

Opening Our Eyes

God totally loves the work of His hands and He created humankind as the pinnacle of all His creative acts to receive His love and to propagate it. His first covenant is with the entire human race and is sometimes called the creation mandate. Love lies at its heart.

First, He authorises that a man and a woman should form a loving, unashamed partnership, enjoying sex and producing lots of offspring after their kind. The ability to reproduce human life is the greatest of God's delegated responsibilities and for that reason the one that should be treated with the greatest reverence.

Second, God authorises Adam and Eve to govern the world. It seems that He deliberately made it a somewhat disorderly place to give adequate scope for human ingenuity and skill! Taming nature is not the same as destroying nature. Although the scope of this mandate was to extend to the whole planet, the Lord set His first people as stewards over a particular garden called Eden.

This was to provide their food, at this time a vegetarian diet. It was also to keep them occupied in creative activity; food was provided on a tree, not on a plate!

There were two special trees within this garden. One was the tree of life, of which Adam and Eve could eat freely. The other was the tree of the knowledge of good and evil. That was forbidden. This was not in order to keep them in ignorance, but so that they might learn about life and the created order through fellowship with God incarnate. This lay at the heart of the garden; God communing with those made in His image.

While Adam and Eve walked in fellowship with God and while they expressed His love for the created order by obeying His mandate, they dwelt in His love. The moment they abused creation they forfeited the right to creation's blessing. Instead, they came under a curse and lost their experience of the love of God. In effect they put themselves on the outside, so it followed, inevitably, that God had to cast them out of His garden.

The breach of this covenant by Adam is the true tragedy of the human race for, as federal head, he has propagated the curse of outsideness to all his descendants. Were it not for the mercy of God and His determination to redeem the human race, the planet would have become uninhabitable. Yet because mercy triumphs over judgment, God has merely made life on earth difficult. And difficult it is. Childbirth is painful; there is tension between the sexes arising from the chemistry of male domination and female desire; food must be sweated from an uncooperative earth and in the end we all die. Worst of all, we have forfeited our right to that quality of intimate fellowship with God that we call eternal life.

Yet God still loves His creation and is determined to redeem it. Eternal life can be restored, death defeated and creation renewed. The promise is given even in the midst of the cursing that inevitably followed the breach of covenant. The serpent will be crushed. One day the Child-Seed of the woman will, in spite of being wounded Himself, utterly break Satan's authority. The prince of the power of the air will be trounced by a greater Prince. There is even a hint of how that would come about. Although Adam and Eve had tried vainly to hide their shame with leaves, God sacrificed animals to provide them with skins.

Discussion Starters

1. Why do you think parts of the Church have denigrated sexual enjoyment within marriage and given the impression that sex was a bad consequence of the Fall?

2. Sociologists often blame our environmental problems on the command to subdue the earth. How would you answer this charge?

3. Education today is secularised. How might fellowship with God improve our education?

4. Adam was the head of Eve and both ruled the animals. Was the reversal of roles – Eve listening to a serpent and Adam listening to Eve – an abuse of God's created order? How relevant is this for today?

5. Original sin refers to the inheritance of bad spiritual genes from Adam. Our modern world believes children are born good until spoiled by upbringing. How would you answer that assertion?

6. Things go wrong. Creation is subject to futility but all things work for good to those who love God. Share examples of this principle in your own life.

7. God's covenant committed Him to save His creation through the promised Seed. Read Revelation 12:1–5. Why do you think the devil hates children?

8. There are only three possible temptations, though many manifestations. What are the most powerful of each one in our contemporary society?

9. Christians move from being 'in Adam' to being 'in Christ'. How does this truth affect your daily life?

10. Adam and Eve lost eternal life. This is restored in Christ. What does it mean to you to have eternal life?

Personal Application

We can commit only three possible categories of sin – the lust of the flesh, the lust of the eyes and the pride of life (1 John 2:16). Eve fell for all three (Gen. 3:6).

When Jesus went into the wilderness following His baptism, He faced the same temptations – and overcame them. Turn stones into bread and gratify your physical desire. See, the world is yours. Just worship Satan! Become a superstar by doing a rope-free bungee jump from the Temple roof.

Since all our temptations boil down to the same three, we can enter Jesus' victory through faith in Him and by drawing on the power of the Holy Spirit.

Seeing Jesus in the Scriptures

Adam is the federal head of the human race. Our first parent defines the spiritual nature of his offspring. We are 'in Adam' and in him we all die. Christ is the last Adam; conceived by the Holy Spirit, He did not inherit 'in Adam-ness'. He is the federal Head of a new race consisting of all those 'in Christ'. They receive the gift of eternal life: restored fellowship with God and an inheritance in the new cosmos that will be birthed at Christ's return.

Adam disobeyed God and ate of a tree that cursed us; Jesus obeyed God and bore our curse on a tree so that we might receive the promised blessing. Concentrate on your life in Christ, you will have little time for the depressing ways of your former life in Adam.

WEEK THREE

Blue - *The Covenant of Providence*

Opening Icebreaker

Each attempt to draw your favourite animal and then see if the others can guess what it is. Then say what creature you wish Noah *hadn't* taken into the ark.

Bible Readings

- Genesis 8:22–9:17
- Isaiah 54:9–10
- 1 Peter 3:18–22
- 2 Peter 3:5–13

Key verse: Genesis 8:22

Focus: God has blessed us with a stable and bountiful planet.

Opening Our Eyes

The fallen world of Adam and his descendants grew so incorrigibly corrupt that God entered judgment mode and destroyed all animal and human life on the planet except for Noah's immediate family and the animals that he took into the ark. When the Flood subsided, God made a covenant in which He promised ecological stability and the preservation of the human species for the duration of earth's existence. This is sometimes called the covenant of providence. God signed this covenant with a rainbow in the sky. It is a perpetual reminder of His providential faithfulness.

This promise allows us to conduct our affairs in a stable world with reliable seasons. The planet keeps its orbit and the poles remain where they are. Climate fluctuations are slow and moderate – in spite of all the talk about global warming. The land is fertile and rain comes in its season. This does not rule out local and periodic ecological catastrophes, nor occasional judgments in particular places, such as Sodom and Gomorrah. Nor does it prevent the disasters that we bring upon ourselves because of our mismanagement of the environment. It does, however, guarantee enough food to feed the entire population of the earth year upon year.

The covenant of providence is for the human race as a whole and so its human requirements are laid on each one of us. Love is at the heart, as with all God's covenants and the conditions are given for our benefit. Problems occur when we or our governments neglect these requirements.

The covenant of providence reiterates the mandate granted to Adam: the great wide world was designed to be filled with people. God's judgment does not mean He has changed His mind about sex and reproduction. Noah's family is to multiply. The human race is also to continue its stewardship over the created order. The animal kingdom is subject to us, so much so that we may now eat meat as well as vegetables. It is worth noting that vegetarianism did not prevent the human race from behaving so badly that God determined to destroy the lot. It takes more than a diet to sanctify the soul.

The one proviso for meat eating is that the carcass should be properly bled; we are not permitted to ingest blood. The reason for this is not only medical but concerns respect for life. This is particularly true of human life, for there is a qualitative difference between us and the animals. In flat contradiction to popular evolutionary theory, we are a special creation, made in the image of God. This is the only adequate foundation for the sanctity of human life. So serious is this matter that God prescribed that life should be paid for by life. In so doing, He took the arbitrariness out of human justice systems; for the first time an absolute marker was set. Murder earns the death penalty; all other crime and punishment can be graduated from this point.

It is impossible to imagine how vulnerable Noah and his family must have felt after the Flood. Everyone they had known had perished, all the familiar landmarks had vanished. The world had been torn apart by vast volcanic action and drowned without a trace. Was there any point in going on? God understood, and once again He encouraged them to repopulate the planet. To further reassure the survivors and the animal kingdom, He repeated His promise never to flood the world again. Whenever we see a rainbow we should thank the Lord.

Discussion Starters

1. The Bible teaches a universal flood and a good case exists for interpreting geology in this light. Secular education interprets geology on an evolutionary model and the media backs it. How would you argue for a Creation–Flood model with students?

2. God has never broken His promise of regular harvests. There is enough food to feed the world, but the distribution is uneven and unjust. What can we do for the poor and hungry?

3. The New Age movement hijacked the rainbow, but it belongs to us! How do you explain the significance of the rainbow to someone on a spiritual search?

4. A vegetarian diet never sanctified anyone. In the light of the bearing of diet on behaviour, what do you make of Jesus' words in Mark 7:15–23?

5. The principle of justice in Genesis 9:6 suggests the death penalty. Why do you think Christians are so divided over this issue?

6. Since the Church is sometimes viewed as the ark of salvation, how do you answer the common objection, 'You don't have to go to church to be a Christian'?

7. Water baptism is the New Testament norm for initiation into the faith. Share together the significance that your baptism holds in your life.

8. The world will end by fire (see 2 Pet. 3:7). How do you feel about the prospect and how do you keep yourself prepared for it?

9. The Flood was salutary but it did not stop the waywardness of the human race. Why do you think that judgment does not cure sin? Is there a better way?

10. People are often fearful of natural disasters. What comfort can you offer to those who worry about the future?

Personal Application

Christians must engage their culture to bear testimony to Christ, but they must not participate in society's sins. They are residents but also pilgrims; in the world but no longer of the world.

In 2 Peter 3 Noah's Flood reminds us that the world will one day end, this time with fire. Christ will return and the familiar created order will be destroyed and replaced by a renewed cosmos.

The complacent world laughs at this prospect. However, believers are to anticipate and hasten the new day by the testimony of their lives and lips. God withholds His hand to allow all who can be saved to be saved.

Are you ready for the coming of the Lord? Are there any adjustments to make to your lifestyle and conduct?

Seeing Jesus in the Scriptures

When Paul preached to the pagans on Mars Hill, he concluded by speaking about justice – God has appointed a Man to judge the world and, in guarantee, has raised Him from the dead. The news provoked a mixed response.

The day of judgment is unavoidable, and Jesus is the human-divine Judge. No one could survive it except that the day of judgment is preceded by the day of grace.

Our standing depends entirely on our relationship with Him. If our faith is in Christ we will be saved from wrath as surely as God preserved Noah and his family. Far from fearing such a day, we should healthily anticipate it, since it will usher in a new world where Christ is owned as Lord and evil is vanquished forever.

WEEK FOUR

Indigo - *The Covenant of Faith*

Opening Icebreaker

Get everyone to describe the best night sky that they can recall and why it was so special.

Bible Readings

- Genesis 12:1–3; 13:14–17; 15:1–7; 17:1–14
- Galatians 3:6–9

Key verse: Genesis 12:3

Focus: God intends to bless the entire human race through Abraham's seed.

Opening Our Eyes

One of Eve's descendants would be the source of redemption, but which one? The line narrowed to the survivors of the Flood. Then, as the population grew, God kept His eye on the family line of Noah's son, Shem. From those descendants He chose Abram. No reasons are given, for God can do as He wills without having to convince us first. The covenant that He made with Abram is totally unconditional.

It was to change Abram's name and his life. He responded in faith to the call of God and became the spiritual father of all those who have faith in the promised Messiah-Christ, as well as the father of the nation of Israel and of all those who trace their descent through his son, Ishmael. He is truly one of the great figures of history and the impact of the covenant of promise is greater today than ever.

There are three parts to the promise. First, a national dimension. The then childless Abraham was, through Sarah, to found a great nation. Second, a personal aspect. Abraham himself, though a wandering Bedouin, would be successful and famous. Third, he would be a blessing to the whole world, with the exception of those who chose to curse his name.

The existence of the nation of Israel today is evidence of God's faithfulness to His covenant. Abraham and Sarah at last conceived Isaac and from him came Jacob and the 12 tribes that were to inherit the promised land of Canaan. Abraham did become very wealthy and his name today is honoured by Jews, Christians and Muslims alike.

However, the most telling aspect of this covenant has to do with the coming of Christ. Jesus is a direct descendant, both by legal title through His adoptive father, Joseph, and (as many understand it) by bloodline through His mother, Mary.

Abraham, with the eye of faith, foresaw the coming of the promised Seed and the redemptive death and resurrection of Christ (John 8:56).

One starry night, God invited Abraham to count the stars and promised him descendants just as numerous. Abraham put his faith in God at that point and it was reckoned to him as righteousness. Then, in one of the most awesome spiritual experiences ever recorded we read how Abraham was instructed to sacrifice animals and to lay the half carcasses in two rows. Then as darkness fell, in fire and smoke, God passed between the pieces and affirmed His covenant.

Later on, God affirmed the covenant again, this time stressing that it was a permanent one. On this occasion He also instituted male circumcision as the sign to be borne by the covenant people of God.

Nehemiah 9 records a great psalm of praise offered as a historical reflection by the returned exiles. Concerning Abraham, they said: 'You are the LORD God, who chose Abram and brought him out of Ur of the Chaldeans and named him Abraham. You found his heart faithful to you, and you made a covenant with him to give to his descendants the land of the Canaanites, Hittites, Amorites, Perizzites, Jebusites and Girgashites. You have kept your promise because you are righteous' (Neh. 9:7–8). An apt summary.

Discussion Starters

1. The mystery about why God chooses some but not others is resolved in Christ, the chosen one. All who elect to enter Him by faith are called 'chosen' and may be assured of their salvation. Discuss this to help those who are uncertain whether or not they are among the elect.

2. Abram's name was changed to Abraham, from 'high father' to 'father of a multitude'. Jesus promises 'a white stone with a new name written on it, known only to him who receives it' (Rev. 2:17). Describe the new sense of identity that Christ has given you.

3. Abraham conceived Ishmael by Hagar in an attempt to provide an heir, though the promised heir would come via Sarah. How are we tempted to shortcut the promises of God in our own lives?

4. God turned Abraham into a nation and gave Israel the land of Palestine. Does Israel still have the right to that land, and how should they handle the Palestinian question?

5. Abraham believed God and it was credited to him as righteousness. He was justified by faith. How would you explain this term to teenagers, and why should they want to be justified by faith?

6. Circumcision is still the covenant mark of the Jewish people. How would you persuade a Jewish friend that circumcision cannot save the soul but only Christ can?

7. Faith is much more than orthodoxy. What difference has trusting in Christ made to your inner self?

8. Many people believe Jesus was a good man and a great teacher but cannot accept that He is the Son of God. How would you persuade them otherwise?

9. Paul describes the Holy Spirit as the blessing of Abraham. What do you think he means?

10. Faith is often tested. Abraham had to offer Isaac as a potential sacrifice, until God intervened. Share some of the tests that your faith has undergone.

Personal Application

Faith is a doing word; it is acting on the assumption that a promise is true. Abraham exercised faith in the covenant of promise before he was circumcised. Salvation is by grace and not race, by faith and not works (see Rom. 4). All who believe that Jesus died for our sins and rose again are justified by faith – true sons and heirs of Abraham (see Gal. 3:6–9). Circumcision is redundant; the death and separation that it represented is fulfilled in the death of Christ. What really matters is the new creation, or spiritual rebirth.

The term 'born again' has been much maligned and misused, but it is still relevant. Have you been born again? If you have, then thank God for the gift of eternal life.

Seeing Jesus in the Scriptures

Jesus took on the religious teachers because of their pride in their legal descent from Abraham (see John 8). True, they were direct beneficiaries of the covenant of promise, but their conduct demonstrated that their real spiritual father was the devil. Thoroughly riled by this deadly accurate charge, they accused Jesus of having a demon. Was Jesus really greater than Abraham?

In an astounding response Jesus claimed that Abraham had seen Him – but Jesus was not yet 50 years old! Jesus said, 'I tell you the truth, before Abraham was born, I am!'

The religious leaders wanted to stone Him for blasphemy. We have to make a choice about Jesus. He is either mad, bad or who He claimed to be – the Son of God.

WEEK FIVE

Yellow - *The Covenant of Law*

Opening Icebreaker

Imagine that you are stranded together on a desert island. Each member of the group writes down five rules that they would make for the community. Then read them out.

Bible Readings

- Exodus 19:5–8; 20:1–17
- Galatians 3:16–29

Key verse: Galatians 3:24

Focus: The law is intended to bring us to Christ and His saving grace.

Opening Our Eyes

Moses is another of those great figures of history honoured by the three major monotheistic faiths. Three months after leading the Exodus he brought the people to Mount Sinai and there God entered into a covenant with the embryonic nation. The Law, as it is commonly known, gave the nation a moral, spiritual, legal, economic and social constitution and it defined it as a theocracy. It consists essentially of the Ten Commandments, accompanied by a wealth of case law and a set of ceremonial rules and regulations to cover the sacrificial system. The entire Law was summed up by Jesus thus: '"Love the Lord your God with all your heart and with all your soul and with all your mind". This is the first and greatest commandment. And the second is like it: "Love your neighbour as yourself." All the Law and the Prophets hang on these two commandments' (Matt. 22:37–40).

Whereas the covenant of promise was unconditional, the covenant of Law comes with the condition of obedience attached to it. The blessing of salvation could not be earned, but to be marked out and privileged to be God's chosen people called for a different standard of conduct to that of the surrounding nations. Obedience merited the favour of God; disobedience brought cursing and judgment. Israel would only survive as a people and retain their inheritance in the land of promise while they walked according to the commandments of the Lord their God. The subsequent history of the nation is really the outworking of this principle.

The Law had four main purposes. It provided the basis for the nation's identity (Exod. 19:5–6). The Israelites could now say that God was their God and that they were the people of the covenant.

It defined sin and justice – morally, spiritually and nationally. Until that point people had understood right from wrong in general terms but there were no definitions of what constituted a transgression nor what an appropriate punishment should be. The Law brought a necessary regulation to human affairs (Rom. 5:13).

The third purpose of the Law was to expose human spiritual impotence (Gal. 2:16). However hard we try, we just cannot keep what we know to be essentially good laws. Indeed, James sees the Law something like a mirror. Throw one stone at it, or throw a hundred; either way the mirror is broken (James 1:23–25; 2:10). We need help!

The fourth purpose of the Law is to bring us to Christ (Gal. 3:23–25). The imagery here is that of a teacher accompanying a student to college and using the opportunity to educate him during the journey. The journey's end is not a degree in law, but a personal encounter with Jesus. The Law has done its job and Christ takes over.

Christ, in His own life, fulfilled all aspects of the Law perfectly, so much so, that even His most acute detractors could not really fault Him. The best they could do was to challenge Him with their own shibboleths, but He could always unmask those for what they were – a cover for hypocrisy. As the One who in all aspects obeyed God from the heart, He became the Author of salvation (Heb. 2:10–12). So, we are saved apart from the works of the Law, through faith in Him alone (Eph. 2:8–9).

Discussion Starters

1. Laws are pointless: the evil don't keep them, and the good don't need them. Discuss this!

2. 'Love, and do as you please' recast as the cynical song 'All you need is love' became the mantra of the permissive society. Situation ethics says there are no absolutes, whatever seems most loving is right. What do you think? Is it a case of love or law?

3. God gave just ten commandments; we have ten thousand. Why do you think this is? What has gone wrong with our society?

4. Israel's national life was governed by a pair of scales: on one side obedience/blessing – on the other disobedience/cursing. In what way do you think Christ threw away the scales altogether?

5. The cross of Christ brought into play the higher law of the Spirit of life. Share some examples of how this higher law affects your daily life.

6. What do you think it means in practice to present 'the parts of your body to him as instruments of righteousness' (see Rom. 6:1–13)?

7. Many people teach that the Sermon on the Mount is an unattainable ideal to which we should aspire. Do you think this is what Jesus intended, or was He giving guidance to His renewed followers?

8. If the Law is meant to bring us to Christ, how would you explain this to a devout Jew or Muslim?

9. Christianity is often viewed as full of repressive rules and judgments designed to keep people feeling guilty. Why do you think we have this reputation and how can we remedy the situation?

10. If the Law brings condemnation, then grace brings liberation. Give an example of how this has affected your own life.

Personal Application

We cannot please God by external conformity to the law. But becoming a Christian isn't a licence for spiritual anarchy. True faith in Christ, genuine spiritual regeneration, changes our behaviour from within. The law of God is written on our hearts in 'Christ-fulfilling' terms; instead of an impossible standard, it becomes a delight. 'Love is the fulfilment of the law', so we instinctively agree with the Ten Commandments. They are the essence of what it means to love God and to love our neighbour.

So great is this inner change that we who died to sin and are risen to new life want to please God. It is not fear of transgression that motivates us, but love for our Saviour.

Seeing Jesus in the Scriptures

The Sermon on the Mount is Christ's great exposition of the true meaning of the Old Testament Law. He did not come to abolish it, but to fill-it-full, to give it its full heart meaning. He proposed a new principle. His followers would live by an inner grace and truth that He enshrined within Himself. 'For the law was given through Moses; grace and truth came through Jesus Christ' (John 1:17).

It is not cheap grace; Jesus took upon Himself all the weight of the law that we had broken. Everyone is cursed under the covenant of Law because not one of us can keep the law, but Jesus bore that curse on our behalf (see Gal. 3:13). The way is then open for us to receive the blessing of His obedience (see Rom. 8:1–4).

WEEK SIX

Violet - *The Covenant of Kingship*

Opening Icebreaker

Invite each member of the group to describe briefly the characteristics of a member of their family tree other than a parent or sibling.

Bible Readings

- 2 Samuel 7:4–17
- Psalm 110:1–2
- Isaiah 9:6–7
- Acts 2:29–36

Key verse: Acts 2:34

Focus: Jesus Christ is rightful Lord over all creation.

Opening Our Eyes

Israel became a theocracy under Moses, that is, a people who leased the land from God, who subjected themselves to His laws and who conducted their lives in tribal regions as clans and families. Itinerant priests and Levites taught the Law and judged issues of law and order. Sacrifices were offered at the tabernacle. At times God raised up military leaders to deliver the people from their oppressors. Prophets brought corrective words that served to bring people back to God's ways. This state of affairs lasted for over 200 years.

Then the people asked the last priest-prophet-judge, Samuel, for a king. He was not happy and nor was the Lord. 'It is not you they have rejected, but they have rejected me as their king.' God told Samuel to warn the people of the price that they would pay. They insisted on an earthly king and He granted them permission (1 Sam. 8); but the experiment was pretty disastrous. A people already wayward now had, with a few notable exceptions, wayward leaders. The prophetic Law of Moses was largely neglected and idolatry became institutionalised. The nation split and eventually went into captivity under the judgment of God.

The Lord did two things during this period. He sent prophets, so that people were not without the voice of God. And He made a covenant with the one king He found to be 'after His own heart'. David the warrior-poet was far from perfect but he never once compromised with other gods. Loyalty and faithfulness, love and devotion, marked him out and as a result God made a covenant with him and, most significantly, with his descendants.

The words of the covenant came through Nathan the prophet. God reiterated His promise of a land for His people. He then covenanted that not only would David's line continue into the temporal future but that it would be an everlasting kingdom. As a result, and in spite of the disobedience of many of his descendants, David's line did continue. All seemed lost when the nation fell to the Babylonians, but the line was restored in the persons of Shealtiel and Zerubbabel when they returned to their land.

However, the greatest significance lies in the promise of an eternal King, the coming Messiah. Psalm 110 is one of many passages that speaks of the Lord of lords and is quoted by Peter on the Day of Pentecost as referring to Jesus. The writer to the Hebrews, speaking of Jesus the Son of God, quotes Psalm 45, making it clear that Jesus is the fulfilment of the covenant promise: 'Your throne, O God, will last for ever and ever, and righteousness will be the sceptre of your kingdom' (1:8).

The fact that Jesus was raised from the dead means that He will never die again. The fact that He ascended to His Father and took His place at the right hand of the Majesty on High means that He is now the everlasting King of kings and Lord of lords to whom one day every knee shall bow. So, in the powerful picture language of the Revelation of John, we find that the government of the cosmos, represented by a seven-sealed scroll, can be given to just one person. 'See, the Lion of the tribe of Judah, the Root of David, has triumphed. He is able to open the scroll and its seven seals' (Rev. 5:5).

Discussion Starters

1. God's people are called prophetically to challenge the world with provocative righteousness, peace and joy in the Holy Spirit. We are salt and light. How can we maintain that keen edge?

2. The Israelites wanted a king, like the surrounding nations. The Bible says, 'Do not trust in princes.' How should this affect our attitude to governments today?

3. God's promise to David affected those not yet born. We want everything now. How can we best invest in a spiritual future that goes beyond our life span?

4. The best stance for the Church is not to govern but to influence strongly. Think of some practical ways that your local church can be an influence for good in your community and local government.

5. 'Christ is Lord of all, or not really Lord at all.' What areas are there in your life that have never really been submitted to the Lordship of Christ?

6. The gospel is primarily about announcing a new ruler and advising people about the terms of His government. Come up with ways that you can most effectively do this among your work colleagues.

7. What are the major areas where Jesus is not acknowledged as Lord in your community? Is there a specific issue that you could take action on as a group?

8. What would you say to those who say that Jesus is their Saviour but who live as though He were not their Lord?

9. Jesus is coming back to claim His inheritance. With all the talk about the end of the world, what is the best way of speaking about the second coming?

10. Jesus taught us to pray for God's kingdom to come. What does that mean in our own situations? It would be good to pray for some specific issues.

Personal Application

The kingdom of God means the government of God. Under the Roman empire, people had to say 'Caesar is Lord.' Christians declared, 'Jesus is Lord.' Sometimes it got them into trouble.

We do not oppose government that upholds good laws, nor are we troublemakers, but sometimes 'We must obey God rather than man'. This applies to all aspects of civic and social life. 'Jesus is Lord' is not just an expression of personal piety. It is a political statement that directly bears on how we live.

It is easy to compromise in an age of tolerance when 'anything goes', but we must stand on the values of God's government. If this costs us, so be it (see 1 Pet. 4:14). Are there areas of compromise in your life? Do you need to speak out for truth?

Seeing Jesus in the Scriptures

Jesus cannot be our Saviour unless He is our Lord. Peter declares that 'God has made this Jesus, whom you crucified, both Lord and Christ.' See Romans 10:9 also.

The apostolic gospel is this: there is a new government, another King, and His name is Jesus. One day, in adoration or in shame, every tongue will confess that Jesus Christ is Lord. This is not negotiable (see Psa. 2:6–7).

The future does not lie with the politicians of the world; nor does it rest in the hands of the devil. Jesus Christ, David's promised Descendant, is Lord. Handel's *Messiah* captures it perfectly: 'The kingdoms of this world have become the kingdom of our God and of His Christ, and He shall reign for ever and ever' (from Rev. 11:15).

WEEK | SEVEN

WEEK SEVEN

Red - *The Covenant of Grace*

Opening Icebreaker

Invite members of the group to testify to one brief example of how the grace of God has touched their lives during the past three years.

Bible Readings

- Jeremiah 31:31–34
- Luke 22:19–20
- Hebrews 8:1–13; 9:13–15

Key verse: Hebrews 8:13

Focus: Christ is the mediator of a better and more effective covenant.

Opening Our Eyes

The Mosaic covenant was good. How could it be otherwise? God Himself ordained it, and it worked. Paul affirms that, because of its convicting work, 'the law is holy, and the commandment is holy, righteous and good' (Rom. 7:12). But there were limitations to this covenant. The problem lay with the people, and for this reason another covenant was required. The great experiment had demonstrated that humans cannot please God by their own efforts.

So, God made a new covenant, one He'd had in view all along, a universal, open access covenant. He did so because of His compassion for us and that is why this is called the covenant of grace. It builds on the past: universal application from Adam and Noah; global blessing through the Seed of Abraham; elect people who delight in God's will from Moses; true spiritual citizenship under David's Heir.

The covenant was launched through Christ. 'When the time had fully come, God sent his Son, born of a woman, born under law, to redeem' (Gal. 4:4). It consists of four major elements. The first is that God will write His law on our hearts. Under Moses the Law had been written on tablets of stone. It was an external force trying with difficulty to access the human heart. All that has now changed. A miracle of spiritual regeneration will occur in everyone who puts their faith in Christ. Ezekiel prophesies: 'I will give you a new heart and put a new spirit in you; I will remove from you your heart of stone and give you a heart of flesh. And I will put my Spirit in you and move you to follow my decrees and be careful to keep my laws' (Ezek. 36:26–27).

The second aspect of this covenant is the right to be the people of God. Peter describes us thus: 'You are a chosen people, a royal priesthood, a holy nation, a people belonging to God' (1 Pet. 2:9). The concept of spiritual nationhood is no longer restricted to the Jews but is extended to all who follow Christ, irrespective of ethnic origin. The people of God are drawn from every nation, tribe and language.

The third promise in this covenant is a direct personal knowledge of God. Under the old covenant people had to be urged to seek the Lord; the new covenant begins with a personal introduction. What other religions vainly strive to attain, we are granted on day one! The Christian faith is primarily about a relationship.

The final element of the covenant of grace is this: 'I will forgive their wickedness and remember their sins no more.' The writer to the Hebrews is at pains to demonstrate that the old covenant blood sacrifices could never really deal with sin. If they could, there would be need for only one sacrifice rather than repeated offerings. However, Jesus offered Himself as a one-time sacrifice and successfully atoned for our sins. The proof of this is that God raised Him from the dead and has seated Him at His right hand.

Guilt causes half our troubles in the world. Peace eludes us while we know that we have offended against God and our fellow humans. The old Freudian trick of denying it or of blaming others doesn't work. The shed blood of Jesus does. Can there be any better news than to hear, 'Your sins are forgiven'?

So powerful is this covenant that the old has been rendered obsolete. From now on peace with God comes only through the sacrifice of Christ.

Discussion Starters

1. The new covenant spells the abolition of religion. What do you think this means and why?

2. God has written His law on our hearts. Share some experiences of how you have found this to be true, especially in contrast to your non-believing past.

3. Imagine you are in the company of a Jew, a Hindu, a Muslim and a Buddhist. How would you explain the idea of a spiritual nation made up of all those redeemed by the blood of Christ?

4. Many Westerners consider themselves non-religious Buddhists. They hope to attain Nirvana and oneness with the Absolute. How might you testify to your present-day personal experience of God?

5. Guilt cripples; forgiveness liberates. In a day when people deny inherent sin but still feel guilty – usually because they are – how would you apply the gospel?

6. God forgives and forgets. Have you forgiven all those who have offended you? Have you forgotten? Remember: love keeps no record of wrongs.

7. The Wesley hymn, 'And can it be', contains the line, 'Bold I approach the eternal throne'. We don't always feel so confident. Discuss some common hindrances to prayer and worship and how we overcome them.

8. What do you consider to be the secret of 'staying power' in the Christian life?

9. The Bible often exhorts us to encourage one another. Share some scriptural encouragements with one another right now in your group.

10. Communion can degenerate into a ritual. How can we ensure the conscious presence of Christ? If your tradition permits you may like to end this series by sharing bread and wine in the name of Jesus.

Personal Application

The covenant of grace guarantees peace with God now and the certainty of heaven, but people will do anything to avoid grace. As followers of Jesus we will make enemies of the merely religious. This can be discouraging. So the writer to the Hebrews urges us to do three things.

First, approach God with confidence. We are welcome in the holy presence through the blood of Jesus. Our praise is acceptable and our prayers will be heard.

Second, remain steadfast in your faith. The Christian life is a marathon, not a 100-metre dash. God is faithful for the long haul and we should stick with Him.

Third, encourage one another. The Christian faith is a shared experience manifested in local churches. Some are better than others and the Church always needs renewal to remain prophetic; yet we should gather appropriately and regularly to encourage each other in God and to stir ourselves up to acts of love and mercy.

Seeing Jesus in the Scriptures

The covenant of grace is profoundly experienced in the Communion. Although the antecedents go back to the Exodus, history took a vital turn when Jesus took bread and wine and passed them among His disciples. As He did so, He announced the inception of the covenant of grace (see Matt. 26:28).

The ratification of that covenant took place only hours later when Jesus was crucified (see 1 Pet. 1:18–19).

Every time we celebrate this simple sharing of bread and wine in remembrance of Him we proclaim the power of His death.

Leader's Notes

Week One: Green – The God of Covenant Love

God bless you as you lead your group! These notes will help you do so effectively, but they are no substitute for prayer and the anointing of the Holy Spirit. The theme of covenant encompasses the entire span of God's purpose for the human race. Such a grand theme requires us to seek Him for grace so that we may help ourselves and others to understand its vastness and relevance for our lives today.

We shall follow the pattern of other titles in this series and suggest that you read the Introduction to the group to help them understand the approach. There are a number of relevant Bible readings. These should be shared out among the group members. If time is a problem then you might like to encourage folk to read the scriptures in advance of the meeting.

Generally you should read aloud the Opening Our Eyes section, the Personal Application and Seeing Jesus in the Scriptures sections before addressing the Discussion Starters. Use others in the group to read these sections. The Discussion Starters mostly arise from the order of the subject matter in the other sections.

Opening Icebreaker

This icebreaker is a fun exercise based on the old business practice of using notched tally sticks to record financial deals tallying. It reminds us that covenants involve at least two parties.

Aim of the Session

We want to get across some profound truth about the nature and character of God. We live in an age when God is often

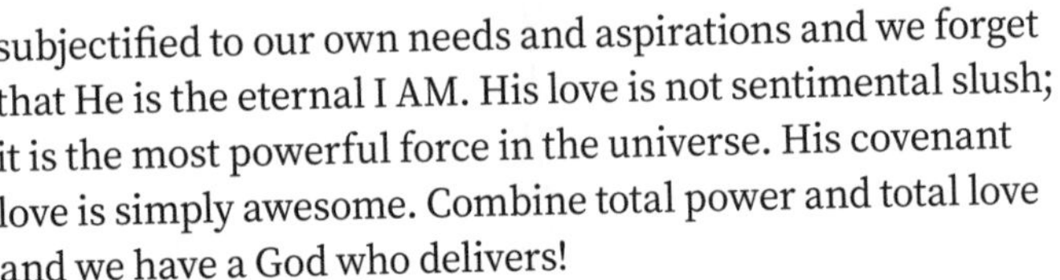

subjectified to our own needs and aspirations and we forget that He is the eternal I AM. His love is not sentimental slush; it is the most powerful force in the universe. His covenant love is simply awesome. Combine total power and total love and we have a God who delivers!

All this is set in the marketplace of a pluralistic society and Discussion Starter 1 reminds us that we have to make our pitch along with everyone else. You will need to speak of God's timelessness, His love, grace and mercy, His justice and truth. Discussion Starter 2 helps you remember that every molecule in the universe is God-breathed and God-sustained.

In our cynical society we do well to see the problem of evil in the context of God's underlying love. We cannot know the full story of other people's lives, or why they suffer. Use Discussion Starter 3 to draw out this point.

God's passion never fails, but ours waxes and wanes like the moon. With Discussion Starters 4 and 5 encourage the group to look at the realities of life and to come up with practical means of renewing spiritual vigour. Sainthood is not the preserve of the spiritual expert. The word means 'set apart ones'. It does not mean walking round with a simpering smile all day! It does mean wholehearted love for God and our neighbours.

Our covenants sometimes fail and never more tragically than when a marriage breaks down. Covenant is important, but even a church wedding does not guarantee that a marriage will last. Like a garden, it must be tended and nourished. Use Discussion Starter 7 to draw out some tips.

Discussion Starters 8 to 10 focus your attention on Christ. He was the greatest recipient of God's covenant love and also the One who saw it tested to the limit. Surely if Jesus could trust

His Father's word of commitment then surely we can too. The notion of God covenanting with Himself will be difficult for some to grasp. Perhaps the nearest we get to it is when someone swears, 'On my life!'

Week Two: Orange - The Covenant of Life

Opening Icebreaker

This little exercise is simply to remind you of the importance of fruit and fruitfulness in the Garden of Eden. Eating the forbidden fruit led to the downfall of the human race.

Aim of the Session

The creation mandate defines the role of the human race in God's great universe. When we obey Him we walk in fellowship with Him and with one another but when we abuse this covenant we are lost.

Discussion Starter 1 serves to remind you that the fellowship between husband and wife expressed in sexual intimacy is a good and God-given blessing. Sex did not arise as a result of the Fall. The Church abuses this truth when it copies the old secular Greek belief that the body is evil. Bodies are good, so are sexual organs and sexual pleasure. All God insists on, for our own good, is that sex is enjoyed in the context of an exclusive faithful marriage.

Classical paintings often show Adam and Eve standing coyly behind strategically placed shrubs apparently with nothing better to do. Discussion Starters 2 and 3 help you to understand that they were given the raw materials to cultivate and to create and that they were to learn the mysteries of the universe at the feet of the Lord. It is secularism that abuses the environment. Christians following the Bible know that we are stewards and not owners, and that we are to nurture

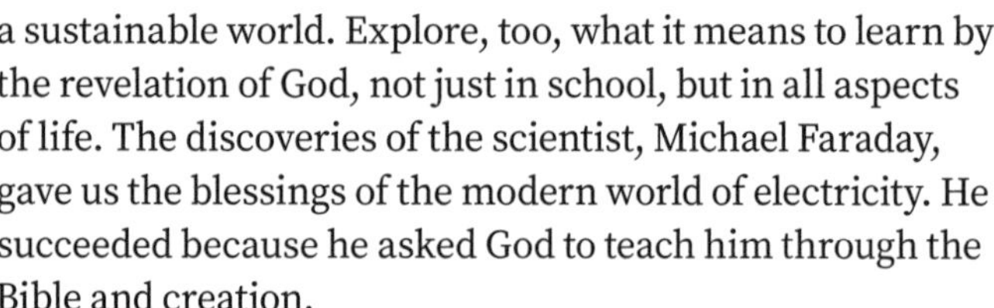

a sustainable world. Explore, too, what it means to learn by the revelation of God, not just in school, but in all aspects of life. The discoveries of the scientist, Michael Faraday, gave us the blessings of the modern world of electricity. He succeeded because he asked God to teach him through the Bible and creation.

The issue of the created order is a controversial one and Discussion Starter 4 will help you explore it! Whatever headship means it does not mean domination and subjugation. You will have to deal with some cultural stereotypes and maybe point people to Jesus as the only Man who got it consistently right.

We cannot avoid the reality of the Fall. The created order is cursed with futility. Things go wrong; accidents happen. Discussion Starter 6 will remind you that God transforms all things for good in the lives of the redeemed. Try to draw out pithy rather than lengthy examples of this truth in people's experiences.

Discussion Starters 7 to 9 focus on Christ the promised Seed, the Second Adam. Read the section on Seeing Jesus in the Scriptures. Our Western individualism often makes us blind to the crucial words, 'in Him'. Our entire salvation is in a corporate context that the visible Church should model.

So important is the promise of the Seed that the devil, it seems, would do anything to prevent Him coming. Is this why children are so often the target of Satan's malice? Yet Christ came and in the wilderness He disarmed the strong man and returned to His society to set people free from Satan's grip. We too must resist the devil. The temptations remain the same, but the window dressing is different in each generation.

Since life was the issue at stake in the garden, Discussion Starter 10 asks you to explain eternal life. It is more than simply heaven when we die. Rather it is a quality of eternal spirituality enjoyed right now through fellowship with God by the Spirit.

Week Three: Blue - The Covenant of Providence

Opening Icebreaker

Most people are familiar with the story of Noah's ark. This piece of fun will just remind us of the context in which God gave His covenant of providence.

Aim of the Session

With all the talk about the environment it is timely for us to rediscover the covenant of providence. There are some overly-spiritual Christians who become so detached from the world that they forget that God not only created but also sustains and provides everything needed for the human race. In short, He cares about the environment.

However contemporary this theme, we must differ with the status quo of the educational and scientific establishment. Discussion Starter 1 confronts you with the challenge of evolution. The issue is not merely academic; this destructive myth wrecks the possibility of faith in the lives of countless young people every year.

Discussion Starter 2 deals with the reality of injustice in the world. Christians are well involved in famine relief but the problem is political and requires political engagement on our part. There are good ways and bad ways of taking political action, but to refuse to act is irresponsible.

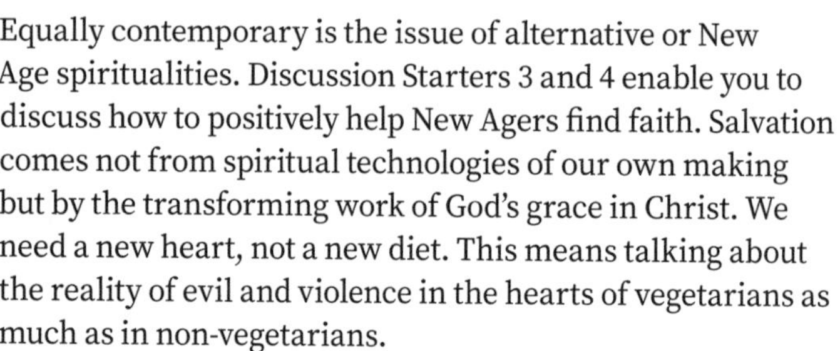

Equally contemporary is the issue of alternative or New Age spiritualities. Discussion Starters 3 and 4 enable you to discuss how to positively help New Agers find faith. Salvation comes not from spiritual technologies of our own making but by the transforming work of God's grace in Christ. We need a new heart, not a new diet. This means talking about the reality of evil and violence in the hearts of vegetarians as much as in non-vegetarians.

That reality leads us to the issues of human justice. Discussion Starter 5 confronts you with the perennial matter of the death penalty. This is a hot topic, often dividing Christians down their left/right political lines. Remind people that we must consider not only the principle and whether it still applies in the light of the Sermon on the Mount, but also the corruptibility of the police and the judiciary. Can the death penalty be justly upheld today, and if so how?

Discussion Starters 6 and 7 raise the issue of the place of the Church in society. Arguably we do not have to attend a traditional form of Church to be Christians. Many people belong to non-formal expressions, such as Alpha groups and workplace cells. However, the faith is corporate and it is not possible to obey the Lord unless we are, as our circumstances allow, active participants in a committed fellowship of believers. When you come onto the issue of how you join the Church, ie the matter of baptism, I suggest you concentrate on its significance rather than the mode practised in your church tradition.

Discussion Starters 8 to 10 focus on the future. The world will end at the return of Christ – with fire, along with the cosmos as we know it. This is a judgment, but it also heralds the renewal of all creation. The threat of judgment does not lead to true repentance. People grow hard in their hearts when things go badly and many blame God rather than turn to Him. It is the goodness of God that leads to repentance. His judgments are acts of justice, they are not meant to convert people. His love expressed through the sacrifice of His Son is what transforms lives.

The challenge of the second coming is for us to be prepared for that day. The future is assured. It is not comfortable, but full comfort can be found through faith in Christ, and this is the encouragement that we can offer to the fearful.

Week Four: Indigo - The Covenant of Promise

Opening Icebreaker

Night skies are a rarity for those living in well-lit cities, so expect holiday or travel reminiscences! Abraham was promised descendants as numerous as the stars, and he could probably see a lot more of them than we can today.

Aim of the Session

With the introduction of Abraham we see God focusing His purpose on a chosen individual in whom He found true faith being exercised in response to His word. It was a pivotal moment in history, for the saga of Abraham and Sarah laid the foundation not only for the Judaeo-Christian faith but for the whole Middle Eastern situation occupying our news media today.

Discussion Starter 1 confronts you with the mystery surrounding the central theme of divine election. Unfortunately, much of Western thought on the subject is conditioned by a deterministic world view which leaves us facing a frustrating contradiction between free will and election. Try to avoid this! It is better to concentrate on the promises given to all those who are in Christ and to stress the security of belonging to Him. This is really the point of

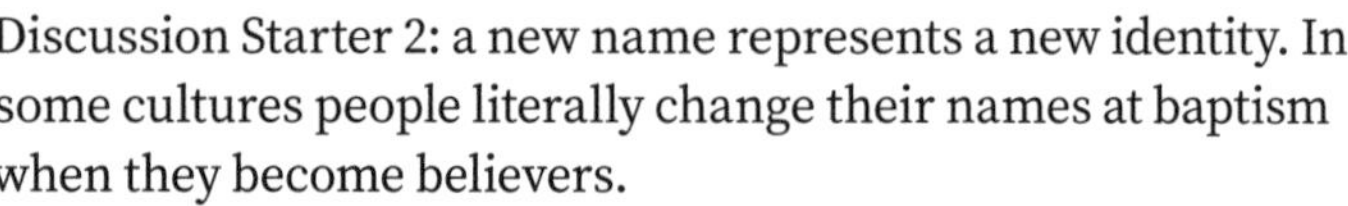

Discussion Starter 2: a new name represents a new identity. In some cultures people literally change their names at baptism when they become believers.

Most of us have some prayers that are not yet answered though we feel God has promised an answer. Abraham made the mistake of trying to find another, carnal way, of producing the promised heir. Sometimes people marry the wrong person because they grow desperate waiting for the right one. Use Discussion Starter 3 to talk about these issues.

Some Christians follow 'replacement theology' which means that all references to the land and to Israel are now spiritualised. Others believe that God still has purposes for natural Israel as a nation. It is a contentious issue but one that we have to explore in the light of international tension in the region. Discussion Starter 4 invites some very contemporary comment.

If you don't believe that God is the Judge of all the earth and that He is angry with the behaviour of us rebel humans, then there is no point in talking about justification by faith. So our starting point in addressing, say, teenagers, is with the nature and reality of God Himself. Discussion Starter 5 invites you to take theological language and make it simple enough for the unchurched.

Discussion Starters 6 to 8 bring you face to face with the reality of salvation through faith in Christ alone. In New Testament times Paul had to contend with the Judaisers who taught that faith *plus* circumcision saved. He and other apostles also had to deal with those whose outer beliefs seemed orthodox but whose lives were dissolute, and with those who denied the true nature of Christ. The issues are still with us. Some in the group may have doubts; all of us have to know how to answer not-yet-believers. We must remember, however, that this comes through the revelation of God and not merely by argumentative persuasion.

Discussion Starter 9 reminds you that faith is always tested by circumstances, not to destroy it but to purify it. We are speaking here of more than the common trials of life. Try to get people to share examples where their faith was actually strengthened through trial.

Paul understands that the gift of the Holy Spirit, the indwelling presence of God in every true believer, is at the heart of the promise. With the aid of Discussion Starter 10 check out the reality of the work of the Spirit in your lives.

Week Five: Yellow - The Covenant of Law

Opening Icebreaker

Putting people together on islands or in a house to see how they relate has become popular TV entertainment. This icebreaker invites us to set our own basic rules for such a community. See how they parallel the Ten Commandments.

Aim of the Session

All nations have laws; only one nation claimed to get its laws directly from God Himself. The Law became the cornerstone of Israel's identity, challenging and inspiring them in equal measure. Today, the issues of law and order are still with us and the extent to which we can legislate for personal behaviour remains contentious in a liberal society.

Discussion Starters 1 and 2 invite you to consider whether there is ever any point in having rules of conduct. You should note that the underlying assumption of both challenges to the need for law is idealism and the belief that somehow, given sufficient freedom, we could develop an ideal society. The

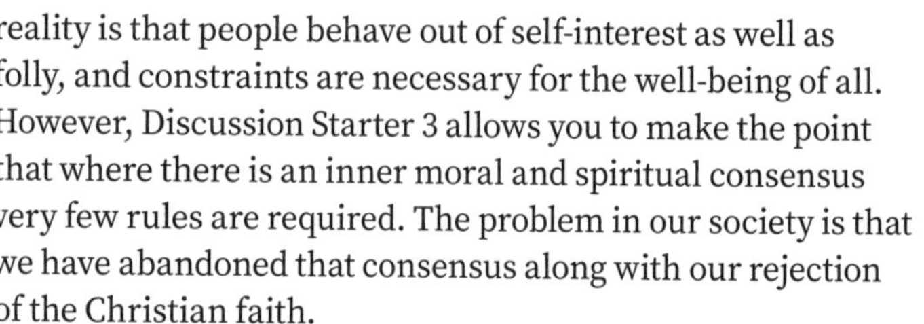

reality is that people behave out of self-interest as well as folly, and constraints are necessary for the well-being of all. However, Discussion Starter 3 allows you to make the point that where there is an inner moral and spiritual consensus very few rules are required. The problem in our society is that we have abandoned that consensus along with our rejection of the Christian faith.

Be good and you receive a reward, misbehave and you are punished, is the common pattern that parents use in raising their children to grasp the difference between right and wrong. Is there a higher way? Discussion Starter 4 suggests that there is, and it has to do with grace and love replacing law. This leads naturally onto Discussion Starter 5 and the place of the Holy Spirit. This is the vital and often neglected key to Christian living. If we obey the prompting of the Spirit and respond to His love, we will behave in a manner that pleases God and blesses our neighbours.

Paul was accused of encouraging licence in claiming that faith supersedes law. He answered that those who died to sin and who were raised to new life in Christ would want to please God and so could be encouraged to offer their bodies willingly to God's service. Use Discussion Starter 6 to remind people that we are not simply looking for examples of dedication to church activities but we want to see a transformed approach to the whole of daily living.

In the Sermon on the Mount, Jesus gave the law its full heart meaning and invited all those who yearned for something better to embrace His path of blessing. Discussion Starter 7 allows you to see that His teaching is eminently practical and possible. With the aid of the Holy Spirit we can treat it not as a new set of rules but as a series of prompts and reminders.

Discussion Starter 8 reminds you that the law is not an end in itself but the means of bringing spiritual children to the place where they meet Christ. It is not necessary to condemn the Jew or the Muslim; simply invite them to travel further along the road.

It is probably true that the Church has so emphasised guilt and sin that people have not appreciated the liberating message of grace that lies at the heart of the gospel. Discussion Starters 9 and 10 call you to share a faith that is more than 'sin management'. You need to emphasise the power of positive living for Christ rather than simply the need to abstain from sin. If we live by the Spirit we will not fulfil the cravings of the self.

Week Six: Violet - The Covenant of Kingship

Opening Icebreaker

Some people won't want to talk about members of their family! In which case ask them to describe someone who has helped them spiritually. Natural or spiritual, we all have ancestors. The covenant of kingship is much to do with the importance of ancestry and descendants.

Aim of the Session

Under the Law the nation of Israel was directly answerable to God and was blessed accordingly. The desire for a king was a mistake but one that proved redeemable in David and the promise of an everlasting kingdom that would find its fulfilment in Christ. Today, Jesus reigns at the right hand of the Father. He is King of kings and Lord of lords and one day will return in person to claim His inheritance. This covenant has practical implications for us as both citizens of this world and of heaven.

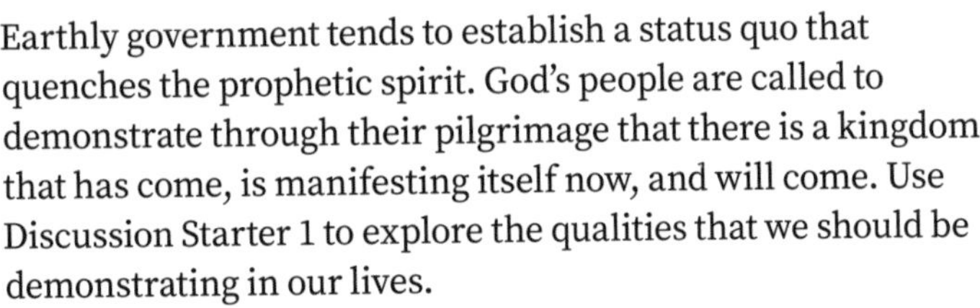

Earthly government tends to establish a status quo that quenches the prophetic spirit. God's people are called to demonstrate through their pilgrimage that there is a kingdom that has come, is manifesting itself now, and will come. Use Discussion Starter 1 to explore the qualities that we should be demonstrating in our lives.

We grow tired of political promises that do not deliver, but still we vote our politicians back into power! Should we withdraw from the political process or should we seek to redeem it? Use Discussion Starters 2 and 4. Your church may already be well involved in the community, but there is always more that we can do. Encourage people to think about the needs that are common to the community rather than just the issues that concern us. Discussion Starter 7 will, however, invite you, once you have addressed the positive issues, to root out by prayer and corporate witness the destructive elements in our society.

Discussion Starter 3 invites you to think beyond your immediate needs and aspirations. Some will tell you that Jesus is coming back so soon that there is no point in the question, but that is not a biblical position. Jesus spoke about investing in heaven, meaning serving others, giving to the poor and spreading the gospel.

There was a time when preachers taught that Christ could be Saviour and later on Lord. That is nonsense. He has to be both Lord and Saviour. Take the opportunity, with Discussion Starter 5, to invite some serious heart searching. Some members of the group may value private counsel and this should be offered. Discussion Starter 8 may help some understand why there is blatant inconsistency in the lives of some professing Christians.

Work is where most of us spend the majority of our time. We are commissioned by Christ to be His presence and voice to our colleagues. Issues about the government often come up in work conversations. Encourage people to use these opportunities to talk about the government of God and its practical bearing on the big issues of the day.

Christians have varying views about the way the world will end. Some of these are plainly sensationalist and speculative. All agree that Jesus will come back. Using Discussion Starter 9 put the emphasis on preparedness for His coming rather than getting bogged down with our reading of the divine calendar.

The Greek word for kingdom is *basileia* and, when used of God's kingdom, it refers to His universal government rather than to a limited piece of land. When we pray for His kingdom to come, we are asking for people to acknowledge Him as their King. Use Discussion Starter 10 to encourage some specific prayer.

Week Seven: Red - The Covenant of Grace

Opening Icebreaker

This last covenant is the one that has most directly transformed our spiritual lives. Use this icebreaker to draw out some encouraging testimonies of God's grace.

Aim of the Session

The covenant of grace is the central theme of the gospel. Within it is enshrined Jesus Christ and His redemptive work and in Him are summed up all the promises of God. It is like no other religion and can properly be called the new covenant because it superseded the old. If religion is our attempt to find spiritual life, the new covenant of grace is God's free gift of spiritual life to all who receive His Son. Who needs religion

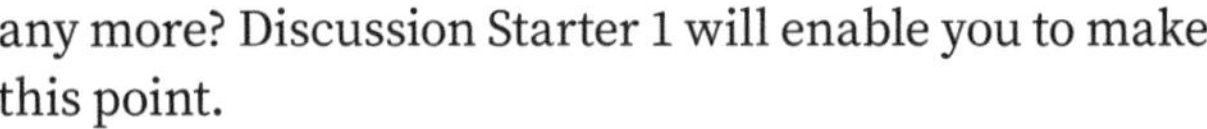

any more? Discussion Starter 1 will enable you to make this point.

Becoming a believer in Christ takes the rules off the page and writes them with a grace script on the heart. We find ourselves delighting to please God; we agree with His will. Sometimes we are surprised at our own improved behaviour as a consequence! Use Discussion Starter 2 to share some of these surprises.

The four great elements of the covenant of grace apply to people of every nation who put their faith in Christ. They become one new spiritual nation. As you consider Discussion Starter 3 it is important to emphasise that the members of this new nation do not have to abandon their own culture in order to believe, nor do they have to become Westernised.

The popularity of Westernised Buddhism, particularly among intellectuals, requires a response from us – the reason for Discussion Starter 4. Where they hope to reach is where we begin! They want to reach the Absolute; we spend our lives exploring the depths of a living relationship with God.

Central to the covenant of grace is the blood sacrifice of Jesus. Jesus made a genuine atonement for our sins and made possible complete forgiveness. Use Discussion Starter 5 to make the point that much modern counselling tries to treat guilt feelings without dealing with the underlying causes. Christ deals with our actual guilt as well as the feelings of guilt.

Jesus taught that there is no forgiveness for those who will not forgive. Use Discussion Starter 6 to help you all check out not only that you have forgiven but also forgotten. Some of us do that but we still keep records! Maybe letters need to be burned and material deleted from computers.

God welcomes us into His presence at any time of day or night. How difficult we sometimes make it. The covenant guarantees our acceptance, but we look at our own failings. Discussion Starter 7 provides you with an opportunity to speak about your devotional lives and to encourage each other in seeking God.

Discussion Starters 8 and 9 touch on the reality of living for Christ in a sometimes hostile environment. We all feel like giving up at times. Even to acknowledge that is liberating. Our problem is often that we are regretting too much of the past and worrying too much about the future. God promises us daily grace, and encourages us to stir one another up to love and good works. Invite the group to share scriptures that build each other up.

Hopefully, as we reach the climax to this group of studies people have a sense that they have grown closer to one another and to God. Discussion Starter 10 invites you to share bread and wine in the simplicity of fellowship and in celebration of our Saviour. Even if you feel you cannot do this it would be good to pray round the group to thank the Lord for His sacrificial death that ratified the new covenant.

Notes...

Notes...

The *Cover to Cover* Bible Study Series

1 Corinthians
Growing a Spirit-filled church
ISBN: 978-1-85345-374-8

2 Corinthians
Restoring harmony
ISBN: 978-1-85345-551-3

1,2,3 John
Walking in the truth
ISBN: 978-1-78259-763-6

1 Peter
Good reasons for hope
ISBN: 978-1-78259-088-0

2 Peter
Living in the light of God's promises
ISBN: 978-1-78259-403-1

23rd Psalm
The Lord is my shepherd
ISBN: 978-1-85345-449-3

1 Timothy
Healthy churches - effective Christians
ISBN: 978-1-85345-291-8

2 Timothy and Titus
Vital Christianity
ISBN: 978-1-85345-338-0

Abraham
Adventures of faith
ISBN: 978-1-78259-089-7

Acts 1-12
Church on the move
ISBN: 978-1-85345-574-2

Acts 13-28
To the ends of the earth
ISBN: 978-1-85345-592-6

Barnabas
Son of encouragement
ISBN: 978-1-85345-911-5

Bible Genres
Hearing what the Bible really says
ISBN: 978-1-85345-987-0

Daniel
Living boldly for God
ISBN: 978-1-85345-986-3

David
A man after God's own heart
ISBN: 978-1-78259-444-4

Ecclesiastes
Hard questions and spiritual answers
ISBN: 978-1-85345-371-7

Elijah
A man and his God
ISBN: 978-1-85345-575-9

Elisha
A lesson in faithfulness
ISBN: 978-1-78259-494-9

Ephesians
Claiming your inheritance
ISBN: 978-1-85345-229-1

Esther
For such a time as this
ISBN: 978-1-85345-511-7

Ezekiel
A prophet for all times
ISBN: 978-1-78259-836-7

Fruit of the Spirit
Growing more like Jesus
ISBN: 978-1-85345-375-5

Galatians
Freedom in Christ
ISBN: 978-1-85345-648-0

Genesis 1-11
Foundations of reality
ISBN: 978-1-85345-404-2

Genesis 12-50
Founding fathers of faith
ISBN: 978-1-78259-960-9

God's Rescue Plan
Finding God's fingerprints on human history
ISBN: 978-1-85345-294-9

Great Prayers of the Bible
Applying them to our lives toc
ISBN: 978-1-85345-253-6

Habakkuk
Choosing God's way
ISBN: 978-1-78259-843-5

Haggai
Motivating God's people
ISBN: 978-1-78259-686-8

Hebrews
Jesus - simply the best
ISBN: 978-1-85345-337-3

Isaiah 1-39
Prophet to the nations
ISBN: 978-1-85345-510-0

Isaiah 40-66
Prophet of restoration
ISBN: 978-1-85345-550-6

Jacob
Taking hold of God's blessing
ISBN: 978-1-78259-685-1

ames
aith in action
SBN: 978-1-85345-293-2

eremiah
The passionate prophet
SBN: 978-1-85345-372-4

ob
The source of wisdom
SBN: 978-1-78259-992-0

oel
etting real with God
SBN: 978-1-78951-927-2

ohn's Gospel
xploring the seven miraculous igns
SBN: 978-1-85345-295-6

onah
escued from the depths
SBN: 978-1-78259-762-9

oseph
he power of forgiveness and econciliation
SBN: 978-1-85345-252-9

oshua 1-10
and in hand with God
SBN: 978-1-85345-542-7

oshua 11-24
alled to service
BN: 978-1-78951-138-3

udges 1-8
he spiral of faith
BN: 978-1-85345-681-7

udges 9-21
earning to live God's way
BN: 978-1-85345-910-8

uke
prescription for living
BN: 978-1-78259-270-9

ark
ife as it is meant to be lived
BN: 978-1-85345-233-8

ary
he mother of Jesus
BN: 978-1-78259-402-4

oses
ace to face with God
BN: 978-1-85345-336-6

ames of God
xploring the depths of God's haracter
BN: 978-1-85345-680-0

Nehemiah
Principles for life
ISBN: 978-1-85345-335-9

Parables
Communicating God on earth
ISBN: 978-1-85345-340-3

Philemon
From slavery to freedom
ISBN: 978-1-85345-453-0

Philippians
Living for the sake of the gospel
ISBN: 978-1-85345-421-9

Prayers of Jesus
Hearing His heartbeat
ISBN: 978-1-85345-647-3

Proverbs
Living a life of wisdom
ISBN: 978-1-85345-373-1

Psalms
Songs of life
ISBN: 978-1-78951-240-3

Revelation 1-3
Christ's call to the Church
ISBN: 978-1-85345-461-5

Revelation 4-22
The Lamb wins! Christ's final victory
ISBN: 978-1-85345-411-0

Rivers of Justice
Responding to God's call to righteousness today
ISBN: 978-1-85345-339-7

Ruth
Loving kindness in action
ISBN: 978-1-85345-231-4

Song of Songs
A celebration of love
ISBN: 978-1-78259-959-3

The Armour of God
Living in His strength
ISBN: 978-1-78259-583-0

The Beatitudes
Immersed in the grace of Christ
ISBN: 978-1-78259-495-6

The Creed
Belief in action
ISBN: 978-1-78259-202-0

The Divine Blueprint
God's extraordinary power in ordinary lives
ISBN: 978-1-85345-292-5

The Holy Spirit
Understanding and experiencing Him
ISBN: 978-1-85345-254-3

The Image of God
His attributes and character
ISBN: 978-1-85345-228-4

The Kingdom
Studies from Matthew's Gospel
ISBN: 978-1-85345-251-2

The Letter to the Colossians
In Christ alone
ISBN: 978-1-855345-405-9

The Letter to the Romans
Good news for everyone
ISBN: 978-1-85345-250-5

The Lord's Prayer
Praying Jesus' way
ISBN: 978-1-85345-460-8

The Prodigal Son
Amazing grace
ISBN: 978-1-85345-412-7

The Second Coming
Living in the light of Jesus' return
ISBN: 978-1-85345-422-6

The Sermon on the Mount
Life within the new covenant
ISBN: 978-1-85345-370-0

Thessalonians
Building Church in changing times
ISBN: 978-1-78259-443-7

The Ten Commandments
Living God's Way
ISBN: 978-1-85345-593-3

The Uniqueness of our Faith
What makes Christianity distinctive?
ISBN: 978-1-85345-232-1

For current prices or to order, visit **cwr.org.uk/shop**
Available online or from Christian bookshops.

Be inspired by God.
Every day.

Confidently face life's challenges by equipping yourself daily with God's Word. There is something for everyone...

Every Day with Jesus

Selwyn Hughes' renowned writing is updated by Mick Brooks into these trusted and popular notes.

Life Every Day

Jeff Lucas helps apply the Bible to daily life with his trademark humour and insight.

Inspiring Women Every Day

Encouragement, uplifting scriptures and insightful daily thoughts for women.

The Manual

Straight-talking guides to help men walk daily with God. Written by Carl Beech.

To find out more about all our daily Bible reading notes, or to take out a subscription, visit **cwr.org.uk/biblenotes** or call 01252 784700.
Also available in Christian bookshops.

Printed format  Large print format  Email format  Ebook format